blockchain rx

Unlocking Blockchain's Potential in Healthcare

william webb

contents

1 / introduction to blockchain technology

overview of blockchain

BLOCKCHAIN, at its core, is a system of recording information in a way that makes it difficult or impossible to change, hack, or cheat the system. It is a digital ledger of transactions that is duplicated and distributed across the entire network of computer systems on the blockchain. Each block in the chain contains a number of transactions, and every time a new transaction occurs on the blockchain, a record of that transaction is added to every participant's ledger. This decentralized database managed by multiple participants is known as Distributed Ledger Technology (DLT).

The inception of blockchain technology is often linked to the person (or group of people) known as Satoshi Nakamoto, who in 2008 proposed it as the underlying framework for Bitcoin, a digital currency, or cryptocurrency. The appeal of blockchain in this context was its ability to offer a high level of security and anonymity while maintaining a decentralized record of transactions.

However, blockchain's potential extends far beyond the realms of cryptocurrency. It's like a multi-tool; versatile and efficient, poised to transform various sectors, especially healthcare. But how exactly does it work? Let's break it down.

1. The Anatomy of a Blockchain

Imagine a blockchain as a chain of digital "blocks". Each block contains data, which varies depending on the type of blockchain. In the case of Bitcoin, for instance, the data includes details about transactions, like the sender, receiver, and amount of coins. Once a block's data storage capacity is filled, it's closed and linked to the previously filled block, creating a chain of data known as the "blockchain."

2. Decentralization: The Heartbeat of Blockchain

One of blockchain's defining features is decentralization. Unlike traditional databases like a bank's ledger, blockchain is duplicated across a network of computers. When a new block is added to the blockchain, every computer on the network updates its blockchain to reflect the change. This means that a single entity doesn't hold the power or control over the entire chain. It's a democracy of data management, if you will.

3. Transparency and Immutability: The Twin Pillars of Trust

Each transaction on the blockchain is transparent and immutable. This means once the transaction data has been recorded, it cannot be altered without altering all subsequent blocks and the consensus of the network. This level of transparency and security is like having a notary public in every transaction but without the paperwork or the fees.

4. Smart Contracts: The Digital Handshake

Smart contracts are self-executing contracts with the terms of the agreement directly written into lines of code. They automatically enforce and execute the terms of a contract when predetermined conditions are met. In healthcare, this could mean the automatic release of medical records to a doctor when a patient agrees, or the instant transfer of funds upon delivery of medical supplies.

5. Consensus Algorithms: The Backbone of Blockchain

Blockchain employs various consensus algorithms to agree on the validity of transactions. The most common ones are Proof of Work (used by Bitcoin) and Proof of Stake. These algorithms ensure that the new data being added to the blockchain is the one and only version of the truth that is agreed upon by all nodes in the network.

6. The Evolving Nature of Blockchain

As we stand on the cusp of a digital revolution, blockchain technology is continuously evolving. From its initial application in cryptocurrencies, it is now finding new uses in various fields, including healthcare. This evolution is akin to the early days of the Internet – we are only beginning to scratch the surface of its potential applications.

Blockchain in healthcare could mean secure and efficient management of medical records, transparent and swift insurance claim processes, and even the creation of new models for health information exchanges.

In essence, blockchain technology offers a new and exciting way to think about how we share information and value in the healthcare system. Its implications are vast and far-reaching, promising to bring more transparency, efficiency, and security to the medical field.

As we progress through this book, we will explore how blockchain is not just a technological phenomenon but a catalyst for innovation and transformation in healthcare. We will delve into its applications, challenges, and potential to reshape how we think about medical data and healthcare delivery.

key concepts: decentralization, transparency, security

As we continue our exploration into the world of blockchain, let's dive deeper into its three foundational pillars: Decentralization, Transparency, and Security. These concepts are not just the backbone of blockchain technology but are also pivotal in understanding its transformative potential in sectors like healthcare.

Decentralization: Democracy in Data

At its heart, blockchain is about decentralization. This concept breaks away from the traditional model of centralized authority - think about how a bank controls financial transactions or how a hospital manages patient records. In a decentralized blockchain system, there is no single point of control or failure. This is revolutionary!

Imagine a scenario in healthcare where patient data isn't stored in a single database controlled by one entity, but instead on a blockchain. Here, the information is spread across a network of nodes (computers), each holding a copy of the entire ledger. This means no single entity has complete control over the data, reducing the risk of data manipulation, loss, or downtime. It also means that even if one or several nodes go offline, the system remains operational and intact. This decentralization democratizes data management and enhances the resilience of the system.

Transparency: The See-Through Effect

Transparency in blockchain is like a glass bank, where you can see every transaction happening in real-time. Every transaction on a blockchain is recorded on a ledger that is accessible to everyone in the network. This level of openness is unprecedented in traditional systems.

In healthcare, transparency can revolutionize how we access and trust medical information. For instance, drug supply chains can be tracked transparently on a blockchain, allowing anyone to verify the authenticity and journey of pharmaceuticals from manufacturer to patient. This not only combats counterfeit drugs but also builds trust among consumers.

Moreover, transparency in blockchain doesn't mean personal information is openly accessible. Rather, the transparency pertains to the transactions or interactions themselves. Personal data can be encrypted and secured, ensuring privacy while maintaining the integrity of the transaction history.

Security: The Digital Fort

Now, let's talk about security, which is arguably the most significant aspect of blockchain. The technology uses advanced cryptographic techniques to ensure that data is secure and tamper-proof. Each transaction is encrypted and linked to the previous transaction, creating a chain of blocks that is incredibly difficult to alter.

In the healthcare context, security is paramount. Patient data, which is highly sensitive and confidential, needs the highest level of security. Blockchain provides this by ensuring that once information is entered into the ledger, it cannot be changed or deleted without consensus from the network. This makes fraudulent activities like altering medical records or making false insurance claims extremely difficult.

Additionally, blockchain employs mechanisms like consensus algorithms (like Proof of Work or Proof of Stake) to validate transactions. These algorithms require network participants to agree on the legitimacy of transactions before they are added to the blockchain, adding an additional layer of security.

The Synergy of Decentralization, Transparency, and Security

These three concepts - decentralization, transparency, and security - work synergistically in blockchain. Decentralization ensures no single point of control or failure, enhancing the robustness of the system. Transparency builds trust among users by making every transaction visible and verifiable. Security, fortified by cryptographic techniques, protects data from tampering and unauthorized access.

In healthcare, this triad can lead to significant improvements. Imagine a healthcare system where patient data is secure, easily verifiable, and not under the control of a single entity. This could lead to more efficient healthcare delivery, reduced fraud, and improved patient outcomes.

As we explore these concepts further, it's important to understand that blockchain is not a panacea. It's a tool, a highly effective one, but like all tools, its effectiveness depends on how it's used. The real power of blockchain lies in its ability to be adapted to different needs and scenarios, offering solutions that were previously unthinkable.

As professionals in the field, understanding these key concepts of blockchain is crucial. They are not just technical terms but represent a shift in how we approach data management, security, and transparency in our systems. Embracing these concepts can lead to more innovative, efficient, and secure systems in healthcare and beyond.

evolution of blockchain technology

This journey isn't just about a series of technological advancements; it's a story of how a radical idea turned into a key driver of innovation across multiple industries, including healthcare.

The Genesis: Blockchain 1.0 and Bitcoin

Our story begins with the genesis of blockchain, which is indelibly linked to the creation of Bitcoin in 2008. Satoshi Nakamoto, the mysterious figure behind Bitcoin, introduced blockchain as the technology to underpin this new digital currency. This first generation of blockchain was designed to solve a specific problem – creating a decentralized digital currency. Bitcoin's blockchain allowed financial transactions to be secure, transparent, and, most importantly, independent of traditional banking institutions. It was a bold first step into a new world of decentralized finance.

Beyond Currency: Blockchain 2.0 and Ethereum

However, the potential of blockchain was too vast to be confined to the realms of digital currency alone. This led to the advent of Blockchain 2.0, marked by the introduction of Ethereum in 2015. Ethereum expanded the scope of blockchain from simple financial transactions to more complex applications. It introduced the concept of smart contracts, self-executing contracts with the terms directly written into code. This innovation opened up possibilities for using blockchain in various fields beyond finance, such as legal processes, supply chain management, and, notably, healthcare.

Smart Contracts and Healthcare

In healthcare, smart contracts can automate and streamline many processes. For instance, they can be used to automatically verify and execute insurance claims based on predefined criteria, reducing the time and potential for fraud. This application of blockchain technology can significantly enhance efficiency and trust in healthcare systems.

The Growing Pains: Scalability and Sustainability

As blockchain technology continued to grow, it faced certain challenges. Scalability and sustainability became significant concerns, especially with platforms like Bitcoin and Ethereum. The Proof of Work (PoW) consensus mechanism, while secure, requires an enormous amount of computational power and energy, raising concerns about its environmental impact.

To address these issues, newer blockchain platforms started exploring alternative consensus mechanisms like Proof of Stake (PoS), which is more energy-efficient. These innovations signify the ongoing evolution of blockchain technology, striving to make it more scalable, sustainable, and adaptable to different needs.

Blockchain 3.0: Integration and Expansion

The current phase of blockchain's evolution, often referred to as Blockchain 3.0, is characterized by its integration into various sectors. This generation of blockchain technology focuses on enhancing interoperability between different blockchain systems and integrating blockchain with other emerging technologies like artificial intelligence and the Internet of Things (IoT).

In healthcare, this means integrating blockchain with medical devices and wearables, enabling real-time, secure sharing of health data. This integration can lead to more personalized and efficient healthcare delivery, with potential applications in remote monitoring, personalized medicine, and proactive health management.

The Future: Blockchain 4.0 and Beyond

As we look to the future, we can envision a new era of blockchain technology – Blockchain 4.0. This future phase might involve the convergence of blockchain with cutting-edge technologies, leading to more sophisticated, decentralized, and autonomous systems. In healthcare, this could revolutionize how we manage health data, conduct medical research, and even how we approach patient care.

The Human Factor: Education and Adoption

An essential aspect of blockchain's evolution is the human factor – education and adoption. As blockchain technology becomes more sophisticated and its applications more diverse, the need for education in this field becomes increasingly vital. For healthcare professionals, understanding blockchain technology is no longer a futuristic skill but a necessity to stay ahead in a rapidly evolving digital landscape.

Embracing Change, Envisioning the Future

Blockchain technology has come a long way from its inception. Its journey from a digital currency platform to a technology that has the potential to revolutionize industries is nothing short of remarkable. As we continue to explore its applications in healthcare, it's exciting to think about the possibilities it opens up.

The evolution of blockchain is a testament to the power of innovation and the relentless pursuit of better solutions to complex problems. As professionals and innovators, we are part of this exciting journey. Our role is not just to witness this evolution but to actively participate in it, shaping how this technology transforms the healthcare sector.

Let's continue to learn, adapt, and innovate as we embrace the transformative power of blockchain technology. The future is not just something we predict; it's something we create, and with blockchain, we have the tool to create a future that is more secure, efficient, and equitable. The journey of blockchain is far from over, and the best chapters are yet to be written. Let's be the ones to write them.

2 / healthcare industry: challenges and needs

current state of healthcare data management

AS WE DELVE into the realm of healthcare, it's crucial to take a snapshot of the current state of healthcare data management. This landscape is complex and multifaceted, riddled with both remarkable advancements and challenging hurdles. Understanding where we stand today with healthcare data management is essential to appreciate the role blockchain could play in its evolution.

The Age of Digital Health Records

The last couple of decades have witnessed a seismic shift in how healthcare data is managed. Gone are the days of endless paper trails. In their place, we have entered the era of Electronic Health Records (EHRs). These digital records have revolutionized data management in healthcare, making patient information more accessible to healthcare providers and improving the overall efficiency of care.

However, the transition hasn't been without its bumps. Different healthcare providers often use different systems for their EHRs, which leads to a significant issue - interoperability. Sharing and accessing patient data across different platforms can be cumbersome and sometimes, near impossible. This lack of seamless integration can lead to fragmented patient care and inefficiencies.

Data Privacy and Security: A Persistent Concern

As healthcare data went digital, it also became a target for cyber threats. Data breaches in healthcare are not just a violation of privacy; they can have severe implications on patient trust and safety. The sensitivity of health data requires stringent security measures. Unfortunately, the current state of healthcare data management often falls short in this regard. Traditional systems, despite their best efforts, are vulnerable to attacks and unauthorized access.

Moreover, regulations like HIPAA (Health Insurance Portability and Accountability Act) in the United States and GDPR (General Data Protection Regulation) in the European Union add layers of complexity to managing and protecting patient data. Compliance with these regulations is non-negotiable, but it's a challenging task for many healthcare organizations.

The Challenge of Data Silos

Another significant issue in current healthcare data

management is the existence of data silos. Patient information is often scattered across various databases and systems, controlled by different entities. This fragmentation not only hinders the efficient exchange of information but also impacts the continuity of patient care. In essence, the right hand doesn't always know what the left hand is doing, and in healthcare, this can be a matter of life and death.

The Burden of Administrative Tasks

Healthcare providers spend a substantial amount of time dealing with administrative tasks related to data management. From updating patient records to processing insurance claims, the workload is immense. This administrative burden can detract from the primary focus of healthcare professionals - patient care.

The Rise of Big Data and Analytics

On a brighter note, the healthcare industry is also experiencing the advent of big data and analytics. The vast amounts of data generated in healthcare are being used to derive insights that can lead to improved patient outcomes, personalized medicine, and better resource allocation. However, the full potential of big data in healthcare is yet to be realized, largely due to the issues of interoperability and data fragmentation.

The Patient's Role in Data Management

Patient engagement in healthcare data management is evolving. With the rise of patient portals and health apps, individuals are more involved in their health data than ever before. However, this also raises questions about data ownership and literacy. Patients are keen to have more control over their health data but often lack the necessary tools or understanding to make this a reality.

Looking Ahead: The Need for a Paradigm Shift

As we navigate the complexities of healthcare data management, it's evident that a paradigm shift is needed. The current system, while functional in many ways, is riddled with challenges that impede optimal healthcare delivery.

Blockchain technology, as discussed in previous chapters, holds promise in addressing many of these challenges. Its potential to enhance interoperability, bolster security, and streamline administrative processes could be the key to unlocking a more efficient, patient-centered healthcare system.

The journey to a transformed healthcare data management system is not a sprint but a marathon. It requires not just technological innovation but also a change in mindset and approach. As we move forward, the focus should be on creating a system that is secure, efficient, and above all, centered around the needs of patients.

The road ahead is filled with possibilities and challenges alike. Navigating this landscape requires patience, innovation, and collaboration. The ultimate goal? A healthcare system that leverages technology not just for the sake of advancement, but for the betterment of patient care and outcomes. Let's keep our eyes on this prize as we continue to explore the transformative power of technologies like blockchain in healthcare.

privacy and security concerns in healthcare

Let's navigate the crucial aspect of privacy and security in healthcare. This topic is not just a matter of compliance or technology; it's about safeguarding the sanctity of personal health information. In an era where data breaches are becoming increasingly common, understanding the nuances of privacy and security in healthcare is more important than ever.

The Vulnerability of Healthcare Data

Healthcare data is a goldmine of personal information. From medical histories to insurance details, this data is incredibly sensitive. It's not just about privacy; the information contained within these records can have real-life implications if it falls into the wrong hands. Identity theft, insurance fraud, and even manipulation of medical equipment and records are just some of the risks associated with breaches in healthcare data security.

Why Healthcare Data is a Prime Target

You might wonder why healthcare data, in particular, is frequently targeted by cybercriminals. There are a couple of reasons for this. First, the sheer amount of personal information contained in medical records makes them more valuable than, say, credit card details alone. Second, healthcare institutions often lag behind other sectors in terms of cybersecurity defenses, making them easier targets.

The Challenge of Balancing Access with Security

One of the biggest challenges in healthcare data management is finding the right balance between accessibility and security. On one hand, healthcare providers need quick and easy access to patient data to provide timely care. On the other hand, this data needs to be tightly secured to prevent unauthorized access. Striking this balance is a delicate task and one that is central to the discourse on healthcare data management.

Compliance with Regulations

In the realm of healthcare, compliance with data protection regulations is not just a legal obligation but a moral one. Laws like HIPAA and GDPR set the standards for how patient data should be handled. They require healthcare providers to implement safeguards to ensure the confidentiality, integrity, and availability of patient information. However, meeting these standards is not always straightforward. The complexity of regulations can be daunting, especially for smaller healthcare providers with limited resources.

Human Error: The Weakest Link

It's important to acknowledge that not all security breaches are due to external attacks. In fact, human error remains one of the largest vulnerabilities in healthcare data security. Simple mistakes, like misplacing a laptop containing patient records or sending an email to the wrong recipient, can have serious consequences. Educating healthcare staff about the importance of data security and implementing robust protocols is crucial in mitigating these risks.

Emerging Technologies and New Threats

As healthcare technology evolves, so do the threats against it. The increasing use of IoT devices in healthcare, for example, opens new avenues for potential cyberattacks. These devices, ranging from wearable health monitors to connected medical equipment, often lack robust security measures, making them vulnerable targets.

The Promise of Blockchain and Other Technologies

In previous chapters, we discussed how blockchain technology could revolutionize healthcare data management. Its features - decentralization, transparency, and security - make it a promising solution to many of the privacy and security concerns we face today. Blockchain can help create a more secure and tamper-proof system for managing healthcare data, reducing the risk of breaches and unauthorized access.

The Role of Artificial Intelligence

Artificial intelligence (AI) also plays a significant role in enhancing healthcare data security. AI algorithms can monitor systems for unusual activities that could indicate a breach, detect anomalies that humans might miss, and even predict and prevent potential security incidents.

The Need for a Culture of Security

Ultimately, addressing privacy and security concerns in healthcare is not just about implementing the right technologies; it's about fostering a culture of security. This involves regular training, robust policies, and a clear understanding among all staff that data security is everyone's responsibility.

As we continue to advance technologically, the conversation about privacy and security in healthcare becomes more complex. It's a continuous journey of adaptation, learning, and vigilance. The goal is to create a healthcare environment where patient data is as secure as it is accessible, ensuring both the efficiency of care and the privacy and safety of patient information.

The path forward requires collaboration between healthcare providers, technology experts, policymakers, and patients themselves. By working together, we can strive towards a healthcare system that not only leverages the power of technology but does so with the utmost respect for the privacy and security of patient data. Let's keep this collaborative spirit in mind as we navigate the ever-evolving landscape of healthcare data management. The opportunities and challenges we face today are stepping stones towards a more secure and efficient healthcare system of tomorrow.

inefficiencies in healthcare systems

Let's turn our attention to the inefficiencies in healthcare systems. It's a topic that touches everyone - from the front-line healthcare workers to the patients, and even the policymakers. Addressing these inefficiencies is crucial, not just for the betterment of healthcare services but also for the overall health and well-being of the community.

The Challenge of Disconnected Systems

One of the most glaring inefficiencies in modern healthcare is the disconnected nature of healthcare systems. This isn't just about the technological aspects, like disparate Electronic Health Records (EHRs) systems, but also extends to the communication and coordination among different healthcare providers. For example, a patient's journey through the healthcare system - from primary care to specialists, from diagnostics to treatment - often involves multiple points of contact, each with their own set of records and processes. This can lead to a fragmented healthcare experience, where important information gets lost in transition, and care is less efficient than it should be.

Administrative Burdens

Healthcare professionals, particularly in areas like the United States, often face overwhelming administrative tasks. These include managing patient records, dealing with insurance claims, and navigating complex billing procedures. The time and resources spent on these tasks are substantial. In fact, it's estimated that for every hour a physician spends in direct patient care, nearly two hours are spent on paperwork. This administrative load not only reduces the efficiency of healthcare delivery but also contributes to professional burnout among healthcare workers.

Inadequate Access to Healthcare

Access to healthcare remains a significant issue, contributing to inefficiencies in the system. This includes geographic barriers, where patients in rural areas might not have easy access to specialist care, and economic barriers, where the cost of healthcare prevents people from seeking timely medical assistance. Inefficient access leads to higher instances of untreated chronic conditions, emergency room overuse, and overall poorer health outcomes in populations.

Overuse and Underuse of Services

Inefficiency in healthcare systems also manifests in the overuse and underuse of medical services. Overuse refers to the provision of medical services that are unlikely to benefit the patient - think unnecessary tests or procedures. This not only drives up healthcare costs but also puts patients at risk of potential harm from unnecessary treatments. Conversely, underuse is the failure to provide services that would have been beneficial, often due to systemic issues like inadequate healthcare coverage or lack of patient education.

The Impact of Outdated Technologies

While technology has undoubtedly improved many aspects of healthcare, reliance on outdated technologies in some areas still contributes to inefficiency. For instance, the use of fax machines for sharing patient records is still prevalent in many healthcare settings. This outdated mode of communication is not only slow but also prone to errors and security risks.

The Role of Patient Education and Engagement

Patients' lack of understanding of their health conditions and treatment options can lead to inefficiencies as well. When patients are not fully engaged in their healthcare journey, it can result in non-adherence to treatment plans, missed appointments, and an overall disconnect that hampers the effectiveness of healthcare delivery.

Healthcare Workforce Challenges

The healthcare workforce itself faces challenges that contribute to inefficiencies. Staff shortages, particularly in specialized fields or geographic areas, lead to overworked staff and longer wait times for patients. Additionally, the mismatch in the skills of the healthcare workforce to the needs of the population exacerbates inefficiencies. This includes both the need for more professionals trained in emerging technologies and techniques, as well as the need for more professionals in primary and preventive care.

The Promise of Technology in Addressing Inefficiencies

As we've explored in previous chapters, technologies like blockchain hold promise in addressing some of these inefficiencies, particularly in the realms of data management and secure information sharing. Similarly, artificial intelligence and machine learning offer potential solutions in areas like predictive healthcare, personalized medicine, and efficient patient triage.

Moving Forward: A Collaborative Approach

Tackling the inefficiencies in healthcare systems requires a collaborative approach. It's not just about implementing new technologies; it's about rethinking and restructuring processes, policies, and patient care models. This involves cooperation among healthcare providers, policymakers, technology innovators, and patients themselves.

3 / blockchain in healthcare: opportunities and advantages

enhancing data security and privacy

AS WE'VE SEEN, the healthcare industry faces unique challenges in managing sensitive patient data. Let's explore how we can fortify this data against the myriad of threats it faces, ensuring its integrity and confidentiality.

Understanding the Landscape of Data Security and Privacy

Before diving into solutions, it's important to grasp the landscape we're navigating. Healthcare data isn't just medical records; it encompasses everything from patient histories and treatment plans to insurance information and even genetic data. This data is not static; it's constantly being updated, shared, and analyzed. The stakes are high; a breach can lead to serious consequences, not just in terms of privacy violations but also in real-world health implications.

The Perils of Data Breaches

Data breaches in healthcare are unfortunately not uncommon and their impacts are far-reaching. Beyond the immediate privacy concerns, they erode patient trust, which is the cornerstone of any healthcare system. They can also have financial implications, both for the individuals affected and the institutions responsible for protecting their data.

The Role of Regulations

Regulatory frameworks like HIPAA and GDPR provide guidelines and set standards for protecting patient data. They're a good starting point, but compliance alone isn't enough. The dynamic nature of cyber threats means that healthcare organizations must stay vigilant and proactive, constantly updating their security measures.

The Human Element

Addressing data security isn't just about technology; it's also about people. Training and awareness are critical. Staff at all levels need to understand the importance of data security and how their actions can impact it. Simple practices, such as using strong passwords, recognizing phishing attempts, and understanding the importance of data encryption, can go a long way.

Emerging Technologies: A Beacon of Hope

This is where emerging technologies like blockchain

come into play. Blockchain's inherent characteristics – decentralization, immutability, and encryption – make it a promising tool for enhancing data security and privacy in healthcare.

- Decentralization: By distributing data across a network, rather than storing it in a single location, blockchain reduces the risk of centralized data breaches.

- Immutability: Once information is entered into a blockchain, it cannot be altered without the consensus of the network, safeguarding against unauthorized changes and deletions.

- Encryption: Blockchain's use of advanced cryptography ensures that data is securely encoded, making unauthorized access extremely difficult.

Smart Contracts: Automating Compliance and Consent

Smart contracts can automatically enforce privacy rules and compliance with regulations. For example, a smart contract could be programmed to ensure that patient data is only shared with entities who have explicit consent from the patient. This not only streamlines the process but also adds a layer of security and trust.

Integrating Blockchain with Existing Systems

While blockchain offers promising solutions, it's not a standalone fix. Integrating blockchain technology with existing healthcare IT systems is a complex process that requires careful planning and execution. The goal is to create a hybrid system that leverages the strengths of blockchain while maintaining the functionality of existing systems.

The Challenge of Balancing Accessibility and Security

In healthcare, data not only needs to be secure but also accessible to authorized personnel. This is where technologies like blockchain need to be fine-tuned to ensure they don't hinder the accessibility and usability of data. The ideal system would ensure that healthcare providers have quick and easy access to the data they need, while keeping it secure from unauthorized access.

Looking to the Future: The Evolving Threat Landscape

As technology evolves, so do the threats against it. The future of data security in healthcare will likely involve a constant adaptation to emerging threats. It's not just about building stronger defenses, but also about being agile and responsive to new types of cyber threats.

Collaboration is Key

Enhancing data security and privacy in healthcare is not a task for one entity alone. It requires collaboration between healthcare providers, technology companies, policymakers, and patients. Everyone has a role to play in protecting sensitive healthcare data.

A Continuous Journey

In the realm of healthcare data security and privacy, we're on a continuous journey. It's a path that requires constant vigilance, innovation, and collaboration. By embracing emerging technologies like blockchain and fostering a culture of security and privacy, we can strive towards a healthcare system that is not only efficient and accessible but also secure and trustworthy.

improving patient-centric care

As we delve further into the transformative impact of technology in healthcare, our focus now shifts to improving patient-centric care. This concept, at its core, is about reshaping healthcare systems and practices to prioritize the needs and experiences of patients. It's a holistic approach that extends beyond mere medical treatments, encompassing every aspect of patient interaction with the healthcare system.

The Essence of Patient-Centric Care

Patient-centric care revolves around the idea that healthcare should be tailored to the individual needs of patients. It's about considering patients as active participants in their healthcare journey, not just passive recipients of medical services. This approach involves understanding patient preferences, needs, and values, and respecting their autonomy and decision-making capacity.

Communication: The Heart of Patient-Centric Care

Effective communication is the heart of patient-centric care. It's not just about sharing medical information; it's about creating an open, respectful dialogue where patients feel heard and valued. This includes simplifying medical jargon, actively listening to patient concerns, and ensuring that patients understand their diagnosis, treatment options, and care plans.

The Role of Technology in Enhancing Communication

Technology can play a pivotal role in enhancing communication between patients and healthcare providers. For instance, patient portals and telemedicine platforms can provide patients with easier access to their health information and facilitate more convenient communication with their healthcare providers. These technologies can help bridge gaps in understanding and make healthcare more accessible, especially for those with mobility issues or those living in remote areas.

Personalized Medicine: A Pillar of Patient-Centric Care

Another key aspect of patient-centric care is personalized medicine. This approach tailors medical treatment to the individual characteristics of each patient. It involves the integration of patient data, including genetic, environmental, and lifestyle factors, to devise personalized treatment plans. This is where technologies like big data analytics and AI come into play, enabling healthcare providers to analyze vast amounts of data to make more informed decisions about patient care.

Empowering Patients through Technology

Empowering patients is a fundamental component of patient-centric care. Digital tools like mobile health apps and wearable devices can empower patients by giving them more control over their health. These tools can help patients track their health metrics, manage chronic conditions, and maintain a healthy lifestyle. Moreover, blockchain technology can give patients more control over their medical data, allowing them to manage who has access to their health information.

The Challenge of Implementing Patient-Centric Care

While the concept of patient-centric care is widely endorsed, implementing it effectively can be challenging. It requires a cultural shift in healthcare systems, moving away from a one-size-fits-all approach to a more individualized, patient-focused model. This shift involves not only adopting new technologies but also rethinking organizational structures, workflows, and healthcare provider training.

The Importance of Interdisciplinary Collaboration

Patient-centric care often requires an interdisciplinary approach. This means bringing together a team of professionals from various specialties to collaborate on patient care. Such collaboration can ensure a more comprehensive approach to treating patients, addressing not just their physical health but also their emotional, psychological, and social needs.

Overcoming Barriers to Patient-Centric Care

There are several barriers to the implementation of patient-centric care. These include systemic issues like fragmented healthcare systems, lack of interoperability between different health IT systems, and the resistance to change from traditional healthcare practices. Overcoming these barriers requires concerted efforts from all stakeholders in the healthcare ecosystem, including healthcare providers, patients, policymakers, and technology developers.

Looking Ahead: The Future of Patient-Centric Care

As we look towards the future, the potential for further improving patient-centric care is immense. Advancements in technologies like AI, IoT, and blockchain will continue to provide new tools and opportunities for enhancing patient care. However, the key to success lies in ensuring that these technologies are used in a way that truly centers around and benefits patients.

Continuing the Journey Towards Better Care

The journey towards improving patient-centric care is ongoing. It's a journey that requires us to continually learn, adapt, and innovate. By leveraging technology, fostering open communication, and emphasizing personalized care, we can move closer to a healthcare system that truly puts patients at its center.

streamlining supply chain management in healthcare

Next, let's explore the intricate realm of supply chain management in healthcare. Often overlooked, this aspect of healthcare is a critical cog in the machine that ensures the delivery of care is efficient, timely, and cost-effective.

The Complex Web of Healthcare Supply Chains

The healthcare supply chain is a complex web, encompassing everything from the procurement of medical supplies to managing pharmaceuticals, and from handling sophisticated medical equipment to ensuring these supplies reach their intended destinations. Unlike other industries, the stakes in healthcare supply chains are incredibly high – delays or errors can directly impact patient care and outcomes.

Current Challenges in Healthcare Supply Chains

One of the primary challenges in healthcare supply chains is the lack of transparency. It's often difficult to track the journey of medical supplies from manufacturers to healthcare facilities. This lack of visibility can lead to various issues, such as supply shortages, overstocking, and even the infiltration of counterfeit products into the supply chain.

Additionally, healthcare supply chains tend to be fragmented, with multiple stakeholders, including manufacturers, distributors, healthcare providers, and regulatory bodies. This fragmentation can lead to inefficiencies, such as inconsistent inventory management, wastage, and increased costs.

The Impact of Inefficiencies

These inefficiencies can have far-reaching consequences. For instance, a shortage of critical supplies can delay surgeries and treatments, directly impacting patient care. Similarly, excess inventory not only ties up capital but also risks supplies expiring before they can be used, leading to wastage and increased healthcare costs.

Technology as a Catalyst for Improvement

Thankfully, technology offers promising solutions to many of these challenges. For instance, the integration of blockchain technology into healthcare supply chains can enhance transparency and accountability. By using blockchain, every transaction or movement of goods can be securely recorded and easily traced, reducing the risk of errors and fraud.

Blockchain: More Than Just a Buzzword

In a blockchain-enabled supply chain, every participant has access to a decentralized ledger, which records all transactions across the network. This transparency ensures that everyone involved, from manufacturers to healthcare providers, can track the journey of medical supplies in real time. Such visibility can be instrumental in preventing shortages and reducing wastage.

Moreover, blockchain's inherent security features can help in combating the issue of counterfeit medicines. Each product can be tagged with a unique digital identifier, ensuring its authenticity can be verified throughout the supply chain.

Artificial Intelligence and Predictive Analytics

Artificial Intelligence (AI) and predictive analytics can also play a significant role in streamlining supply chain processes. AI algorithms can analyze vast amounts of data to predict trends, anticipate supply needs, and optimize inventory levels. This means healthcare facilities can have the right amount of supplies when they need them, reducing both shortages and overstocking.

Internet of Things (IoT) in Supply Chain Management

The Internet of Things (IoT) brings a new dimension to supply chain management. IoT devices, such as smart sensors and RFID tags, can track the condition and movement of supplies in real-time. This is particularly important for sensitive items like vaccines, which need to be stored at specific temperatures. With IoT, any deviations from required conditions can be immediately detected and addressed.

Overcoming Implementation Challenges

While the potential of these technologies is immense, their implementation is not without challenges. Integrating new technologies into existing systems can be costly and complex. There's also the need for skilled personnel who can manage and interpret the data these technologies provide.

Furthermore, collaboration is key. A blockchain or an AI system is most effective when all participants in the supply chain are on board and using the system effectively. Achieving this level of collaboration requires not just technological integration but also a cultural shift towards more open and cooperative practices.

Training and Education: Equipping the Workforce

An essential part of streamlining supply chain management is training and education. Healthcare professionals, along with supply chain managers, need to be educated about the benefits and workings of these technologies. Understanding how to use these tools effectively can lead to more informed decisions and better management of resources.

The Future of Healthcare Supply Chains

Looking ahead, the future of healthcare supply chains seems poised for significant transformation. The continued advancement and integration of technologies like blockchain, AI, and IoT promise not just incremental improvements, but a complete overhaul of how healthcare supply chains operate.

As we continue to navigate the complexities of healthcare, let's keep in mind that the goal of streamlining supply chain management is not just about efficiency or cost savings. It's about ensuring that healthcare providers have the resources they need to offer the best possible care to patients. Every improvement in the supply chain, therefore, is a step towards better, more reliable, and more accessible healthcare for everyone.

4 / examples: blockchain applications in healthcare

patient data management

AS WE CONTINUE to navigate through the intersection of healthcare and technology, let's delve into the vital aspect of patient data management. In the realm of healthcare, managing patient data is not just a logistical task; it's an ethical imperative. Every piece of data represents a human life, and how we handle this data can have profound implications on patient care and outcomes.

The Evolution of Patient Data Management

Traditionally, patient data was managed through paper records – a system fraught with challenges such as accessibility, safety, and efficiency. The advent of Electronic Health Records (EHRs) marked a significant leap forward, digitizing patient information and improving accessibility. However, this digital transformation also brought new challenges in terms of data security, privacy, and interoperability.

Interoperability: The Cornerstone of Effective Data Management

One of the biggest challenges in patient data management is interoperability – the ability of different IT systems and software applications to communicate, exchange data, and use the information that has been exchanged. In an ideal world, patient data should flow seamlessly between primary care doctors, specialists, hospitals, and other healthcare providers, ensuring comprehensive and coordinated care. However, the reality often falls short, with data silos and incompatible systems leading to fragmented care.

The Promise of Blockchain in Patient Data Management

This is where blockchain technology can be a game-changer. By creating a decentralized and immutable ledger of patient data, blockchain can provide a secure, comprehensive, and accessible record of patient information. This technology has the potential to solve many of the interoperability challenges by allowing different systems to access and update patient data securely and in real-time.

Data Security and Privacy: A Top Priority

In the digital age, data security and privacy are paramount. Patient data is highly sensitive, and any breach can have serious consequences. Blockchain's encryption and secure data sharing mechanisms offer a higher level of security compared to traditional data management systems. Moreover, the immutable nature of blockchain ensures that once information is recorded, it cannot be altered or deleted, which adds an extra layer of protection against data tampering.

Empowering Patients with Their Data

Another key aspect of patient data management is giving patients control over their data. Blockchain can empower patients by giving them ownership of their health data. Through blockchain, patients can have a more active role in their healthcare, deciding who gets access to their data and for what purpose. This not only enhances patient autonomy but also fosters trust between patients and healthcare providers.

The Role of Artificial Intelligence

Artificial Intelligence (AI) can also play a significant role in patient data management. AI algorithms can analyze large datasets to identify patterns, predict health risks, and suggest personalized treatment plans. However, the effective use of AI in healthcare hinges on the availability of comprehensive, accurate, and up-to-date patient data.

Overcoming the Digital Divide

While technology offers incredible opportunities for improving patient data management, it also raises the issue of the digital divide. Not all patients have equal access to digital technologies, which can create disparities in healthcare. Addressing this digital divide is crucial to ensure that technological advancements in patient data management benefit everyone, not just a select few.

The Challenge of Change Management

Integrating new technologies like blockchain and AI into existing healthcare systems is not just a technical challenge; it's a change management challenge. It requires training healthcare professionals, rethinking workflows, and sometimes, changing the very culture of how healthcare is delivered. This process can be slow and complex, but it is essential for the successful implementation of advanced patient data management systems.

A Collaborative Approach

Effective patient data management requires collaboration across various sectors – healthcare providers, technology companies, policymakers, and patients themselves. It's a multifaceted effort that involves not only implementing new technologies but also ensuring regulatory compliance, addressing ethical considerations, and fostering a culture of innovation and continuous improvement.

Looking Forward: The Future of Patient Data Management

As we look to the future, the landscape of patient data management is set to evolve continually. Technologies like blockchain and AI will likely become more integrated into healthcare, offering new ways to manage patient data more efficiently, securely, and patient-centrically.

drug traceability and safety

Let's turn our attention to a crucial aspect of healthcare - drug traceability and safety. The journey of a drug from its manufacturing to the hands of patients is complex and critical. Ensuring the safety and authenticity of medications is not just a regulatory requirement; it's a matter of life and health.

The Complex Path of Pharmaceuticals

Consider the journey of a medication. It begins in a manufacturing facility, travels through various distributors, possibly across international borders, and ends up in pharmacies, hospitals, or directly with patients. Each step in this process presents potential risks – from manufacturing errors to counterfeit drugs entering the supply chain.

Challenges in Drug Traceability

One of the major challenges in ensuring drug safety is traceability. With the global nature of pharmaceutical supply chains, tracking the journey of a medication can be daunting. There are numerous handoffs, and each transfer is a potential point of failure. Inconsistencies in documentation, human error, or intentional tampering can all lead to serious safety concerns.

Counterfeit Medications: A Growing Concern

Counterfeit drugs are a significant issue in the pharmaceutical industry. These fraudulent medicines may contain incorrect doses, wrong ingredients, or no active ingredients at all. Not only do they pose a direct risk to patient health, but they also undermine trust in healthcare systems and pharmaceutical companies.

The Role of Technology in Ensuring Drug Safety

This is where technology, particularly blockchain, can play a transformative role. Blockchain's ability to provide a transparent, immutable ledger is ideal for tracking the movement of drugs across the supply chain.

Blockchain: A Game Changer in Drug Traceability

With blockchain, each transaction in the supply chain can be recorded in a way that is transparent and unalterable. This means that from the moment a drug is manufactured, its journey can be tracked in real-time. Such traceability not only helps in ensuring the authenticity of drugs but also aids in quickly identifying and addressing any issues in the supply chain.

Combating Counterfeits with Digital Serialization

Digital serialization is another technology that, combined with blockchain, can significantly enhance drug safety. Each drug package can be assigned a unique serial number, recorded on the blockchain. This serial number can then be used to verify the authenticity of the drug at each stage of its journey, all the way to the patient.

Leveraging AI for Quality Control

Artificial Intelligence (AI) can also contribute significantly to drug safety. AI algorithms can analyze patterns in data to identify potential issues in the manufacturing process or supply chain that might compromise drug quality. AI can also be used to monitor and analyze reports of adverse drug reactions, providing valuable insights for improving drug safety.

The Internet of Things (IoT) for Monitoring

The Internet of Things (IoT) can enhance drug safety monitoring. For example, smart sensors can track the storage conditions of drugs, ensuring that they are kept at the right temperature and humidity levels throughout the supply chain. This is particularly important for sensitive medications like vaccines.

Collaboration Across the Board

Ensuring drug traceability and safety requires collaboration across various sectors – pharmaceutical companies, regulatory bodies, technology providers, healthcare professionals, and patients. Each stakeholder plays a critical role in this ecosystem.

Regulatory Compliance and Global Standards

In the realm of drug traceability and safety, regulatory compliance is key. Regulations like the Drug Supply Chain Security Act (DSCSA) in the United States set standards for the tracking and tracing of prescription drugs. These regulations aim to protect consumers from exposure to drugs that may be counterfeit, stolen, contaminated, or otherwise harmful.

Education and Awareness

An often-overlooked aspect of drug safety is education and awareness. Healthcare professionals and patients need to be educated about the risks of counterfeit drugs and the importance of drug traceability. Patients, in particular, should be encouraged to be vigilant about the medications they receive and to report any suspicions of counterfeit drugs.

Challenges in Implementation

While the potential of technology in enhancing drug traceability and safety is immense, the challenges in implementation cannot be overlooked. Integrating new technologies into existing systems can be complex and costly. There is also the challenge of ensuring that these technologies are adopted globally, across a very diverse and fragmented healthcare and pharmaceutical landscape.

Looking Forward

As we look to the future, the role of technology in drug traceability and safety is poised to grow. Innovations in blockchain, AI, IoT, and other technologies offer exciting possibilities for making the pharmaceutical supply chain more transparent, secure, and efficient.

clinical trials and research data integrity

Clinical trials are the bedrock of modern medicine. They are how we test new treatments, drugs, and medical devices to ensure they are effective and safe for public use.

However, the integrity of these trials hinges on the quality and reliability of the data collected.

Data Integrity: The Heart of Reliable Research

Data integrity in clinical trials means ensuring that the data collected is accurate, complete, and reliable. It's about having a clear, traceable record of every piece of data, from patient recruitment to final results. This is crucial because decisions that affect patient health and future medical practices depend on this data.

Challenges in Maintaining Data Integrity

Maintaining data integrity in clinical trials is fraught with challenges. Human error, data tampering, and inconsistencies in data collection are just a few. Moreover, as clinical trials become more global and complex, managing and monitoring this data becomes increasingly difficult.

The Threat of Data Falsification and Mismanagement

Data falsification or mismanagement can have dire consequences. It can lead to incorrect conclusions about a drug's efficacy or safety, potentially putting patients at risk. This is why maintaining the integrity of research data is not just a scientific necessity but also a moral obligation.

Blockchain: A Potential Game Changer

Blockchain technology, which we've seen can revolutionize data management in healthcare, also holds significant promise for clinical trials. Its ability to create a tamper-proof, time-stamped record of data makes it an ideal tool for enhancing data integrity in clinical research.

Enhancing Transparency and Traceability

With blockchain, every piece of data in a clinical trial can be securely recorded and easily verified. This enhances transparency and traceability, making it easier to audit and review research data. This level of transparency is essential not just for the validity of the trial but also for maintaining public trust in medical research.

The Role of Smart Contracts in Clinical Trials

Smart contracts can automate and streamline various aspects of clinical trials. For example, they can be used to manage patient consent, ensuring that participants have agreed to the specific terms and conditions of the trial. They can also be employed to release funding based on the achievement of certain milestones, ensuring efficient use of resources.

AI and Big Data: Enhancing Data Analysis

Artificial intelligence (AI) and big data can significantly enhance the analysis of clinical trial data. AI algorithms can process large volumes of data quickly and identify patterns or anomalies that might be missed by human researchers. This can lead to more accurate results and faster conclusions.

The Challenge of Integration and Adoption

Integrating these technologies into existing clinical trial frameworks is not without challenges. There's the cost of implementation, the need for technological infrastructure, and the resistance to change from traditional practices

Additionally, there's the need to ensure that these technologies are used in a way that respects participant privacy and adheres to regulatory requirements.

Respecting Participant Privacy

In clinical trials, participant privacy is paramount. Technologies like blockchain can help protect participant data while maintaining the integrity of the trial. However, it's crucial to balance the need for data transparency with the right to privacy.

Collaboration and Standardization

Effective use of technology in clinical trials requires collaboration across various sectors – healthcare providers, researchers, technology experts, and regulatory bodies. Standardizing processes and protocols is essential to ensure that the data collected is consistent, reliable, and comparable across different trials.

Ethical Considerations and Regulatory Compliance

Ethical considerations and regulatory compliance are central to clinical trials. Using technologies like blockchain and AI must be guided by ethical principles and comply with regulations like the Good Clinical Practice (GCP) guidelines. Ensuring that these technologies are used ethically and responsibly is critical to maintaining public trust in medical research.

Preparing for the Future

As we look to the future, the landscape of clinical trials is set to evolve with the integration of advanced technologies. This evolution holds the promise of more efficient, transparent, and reliable clinical research.

A Journey of Continuous Learning and Improvement

In the realm of clinical trials and research data integrity, we are on a journey of continuous learning and improvement. By leveraging technologies like blockchain and AI, we can enhance the way we conduct clinical trials, making them more efficient, transparent, and trustworthy.

5 / technical aspects of implementing blockchain in healthcare

understanding smart contracts

AS WE WEAVE through the intricate tapestry of healthcare and technology, let's pause to focus on a fascinating and pivotal concept: smart contracts. While the term might conjure images of legal documents brimming with jargon, in the world of blockchain, it represents a dynamic and transformative tool. So, let's demystify smart contracts and explore how they're reshaping interactions and transactions in the healthcare sector.

The Genesis of Smart Contracts

The idea of smart contracts was first proposed in the 1990s, but it's blockchain technology that has truly brought them to life. At their core, smart contracts are self-executing contracts with the terms of the agreement directly written into code. They are programs that run on a blockchain network, where they operate autonomously, objectively, and transparently.

How Do Smart Contracts Work?

Imagine a vending machine: you select a product, pay the required amount, and the machine automatically dispenses your choice. There's no need for a human intermediary to ensure the transaction is completed. Smart contracts work similarly in the digital world. When certain pre-defined conditions are met, they automatically execute the agreed-upon actions.

The Power of Automation and Precision

In healthcare, smart contracts can automate and streamline numerous processes. For instance, they could be programmed to release medical records to a healthcare provider once a patient provides digital consent. Or, consider a research trial where participant consent and data collection can be managed efficiently and transparently through smart contracts.

Enhancing Transparency and Trust

One of the greatest advantages of smart contracts is their ability to foster transparency and trust. In a sector where these values are paramount, smart contracts offer a way to conduct transactions and interactions that are open and verifiable by all parties involved.

Smart Contracts and Patient Data

Smart contracts can revolutionize how patient data is managed and shared. With their help, data access and exchange can be securely controlled, respecting patient privacy while facilitating necessary data sharing for treatment or research.

Efficiency in Insurance Claims

In the realm of health insurance, smart contracts can automate claims processing, reducing paperwork and speeding up reimbursement. They could validate claims against policy terms and automatically process payments, minimizing fraud and administrative overhead.

The Challenge of Integration

Integrating smart contracts into existing healthcare systems isn't without challenges. Interoperability with current IT systems, ensuring compliance with healthcare regulations, and addressing the digital divide are crucial considerations.

The Evolution of Contract Law

Smart contracts also pose interesting questions for traditional contract law. How do we deal with disputes arising from smart contract transactions? How do we ensure that these digital contracts comply with legal standards? These are questions that legal experts and technologists are actively exploring.

Educating Stakeholders

For smart contracts to be effective, stakeholders in healthcare – from providers to patients – need to understand how they work and trust the technology. Education and transparency are key to achieving this.

Security: A Double-Edged Sword

While smart contracts offer enhanced security, they are not immune to risks. The code is only as good as its creator; coding errors can lead to vulnerabilities. Ensuring that smart contracts are secure, and that there are mechanisms for addressing and correcting errors, is critical.

Potential and Limitations

The potential of smart contracts in healthcare is immense. They can bring about more efficient, transparent, and patient-centered care. However, it's also important to recognize their limitations. They are tools that operate within the broader context of healthcare systems, regulations, and human interactions.

Preparing for a Smart Contract-Enabled Future

As we prepare for a future where smart contracts become integral to healthcare systems, it's important to approach this transition thoughtfully. Balancing technological innovation with ethical considerations, data security, and patient rights is essential.

The Road Ahead

The journey towards fully integrating smart contracts into healthcare is an exciting one. It promises to bring about more streamlined operations, enhanced patient empowerment, and a new level of transparency in healthcare transactions.

integration with existing healthcare it systems

Having delved into the world of smart contracts, let's now shift our focus to another critical aspect: integrating these emerging technologies with existing healthcare IT systems. This integration is not just a technical challenge but a pivotal step in revolutionizing healthcare delivery and management.

The Landscape of Current Healthcare IT Systems

To understand the challenge of integration, we first need to appreciate the landscape of current healthcare IT systems. These systems are incredibly diverse, ranging from electronic health records (EHRs) and patient management systems to more complex diagnostic and monitoring tools. They are the backbone of modern healthcare, facilitating everything from patient data storage to clinical decision-making.

The Heterogeneity Challenge

One of the main challenges in integration is the heterogeneity of these systems. Different healthcare providers often use different IT systems, each with its own set of protocols, data formats, and interfaces. This diversity can create significant barriers to seamless integration of new technologies like blockchain and AI.

Understanding Interoperability

Interoperability is the ability of different IT systems and

software applications to communicate, exchange data, and use the information that has been exchanged. It's a crucial component for successful integration. Without interoperability, even the most advanced technological solutions can become isolated and underutilized.

Integrating Blockchain into Existing Systems

Integrating blockchain into existing healthcare IT systems means ensuring that it can effectively communicate and exchange data with these systems. This involves addressing technical issues such as data formats and protocols, as well as ensuring compliance with healthcare standards and regulations.

The Role of APIs

Application Programming Interfaces (APIs) play a crucial role in this integration process. They act as intermediaries, allowing different software systems to interact and communicate. Developing robust APIs that can interface blockchain platforms with existing healthcare IT systems is key to successful integration.

Ensuring Data Security and Compliance

When integrating new technologies, ensuring data security and compliance with regulations like HIPAA is paramount. Blockchain's inherent security features are a boon, but they must be aligned with the existing security protocols of healthcare IT systems.

The Challenge of Legacy Systems

Another hurdle is the presence of legacy systems in

healthcare. These older systems, while still functional, may not be equipped to handle the demands of newer technologies like blockchain. Upgrading or adapting these systems is often necessary but can be resource-intensive.

User Training and Adoption

The integration of new technologies is not just a technical process; it involves the people who will use these systems. Training healthcare professionals to use these integrated systems effectively is crucial. User adoption is often a bigger challenge than the technical integration itself.

The Benefits of Successful Integration

Despite these challenges, the benefits of successful integration are manifold. It can lead to more efficient healthcare delivery, better patient outcomes, and a significant reduction in healthcare costs. For instance, integrating blockchain with EHRs can enhance data security, patient privacy, and streamline the sharing of patient data among providers.

Collaboration Across Sectors

Successful integration requires collaboration across various sectors - healthcare providers, technology developers, policymakers, and regulatory bodies. Each sector plays a crucial role in addressing the technical, regulatory, and practical aspects of integration.

The Future of Healthcare IT Systems

Looking ahead, the future of healthcare IT systems is

one of greater interconnectivity and interoperability. Technologies like blockchain, AI, and IoT will likely become integral components of these systems, driving innovations in patient care and healthcare management.

addressing scalability and performance issues

As we journey further into the integration of innovative technologies in healthcare, it's crucial to address a pivotal challenge: scalability and performance issues. Whether we're discussing blockchain, AI, or any other advanced technology, their ability to scale and perform efficiently is essential for their success in the dynamic and demanding environment of healthcare.

The Scalability Challenge in Healthcare Technology

Scalability in healthcare technology refers to the ability of a system to handle growing amounts of work or to be enlarged to accommodate that growth. In the context of healthcare, this means the technology must be able to support an increasing number of users, transactions, and data without compromising on performance or efficiency.

Performance: The Make-or-Break Factor

Performance, closely tied to scalability, is about the system's ability to process transactions or data requests within a reasonable amount of time. In healthcare, where decisions can often be time-sensitive, high-performance technology systems are not just a luxury, they're a necessity.

Blockchain: Addressing the Elephant in the Room

Blockchain technology, while revolutionary, faces significant scalability and performance challenges. The decentralized nature of blockchain, which is a boon for security and transparency, can be a hurdle for scalability. For example, the more nodes there are in a blockchain network, the longer it can take to process and validate transactions.

The Issue with Current Consensus Mechanisms

Current consensus mechanisms like Proof of Work (PoW) are energy-intensive and can slow down transaction processing times. This is particularly problematic in healthcare, where delays can have real-world consequences. Finding more efficient consensus mechanisms is a key area of focus in the evolution of blockchain technology.

Artificial Intelligence: Balancing the Load

Artificial Intelligence, another pillar of modern healthcare technology, also faces its own scalability challenges. AI models, especially those involved in deep learning, require significant computational power. As these models grow in complexity, ensuring they can still function efficiently and provide timely insights is crucial.

Big Data: The More, The Merrier?

The healthcare industry is also grappling with the challenges of managing big data. The more data the system has to process, the more strain it puts on the system's performance. This is especially relevant when considering the integration of IoT devices in healthcare, which continuously generate vast amounts of data.

Strategies for Enhancing Scalability and Performance

1. Optimizing Algorithms and Data Structures: One way to address scalability and performance issues is by optimizing the algorithms and data structures used in these technologies. This might mean developing more efficient ways to store and retrieve data or designing algorithms that require less computational power.

2. Cloud Computing and Distributed Systems: Leveraging cloud computing and distributed systems can help. By distributing the workload across multiple servers or nodes, we can enhance the system's ability to handle large volumes of data and transactions.

3. Upgrading Infrastructure: Regularly upgrading the technological infrastructure to keep up with the demands of advanced healthcare technologies is also critical. This includes investing in faster processors, more robust servers, and better networking equipment.

4. Load Balancing: Implementing load balancing, which distributes workloads across multiple computing resources, can enhance the performance of healthcare IT systems. This ensures no single server or node bears too much burden.

5. Hybrid Models: For blockchain, considering hybrid models that combine the best aspects of centralized and decentralized systems can offer a middle ground, balancing the benefits of decentralization with the efficiency of centralized systems.

6. Adaptive AI Models: Developing AI models that can adapt to different scales of data and computational resources can help maintain performance without requiring constant upgrades to hardware.

The Human Aspect of Scalability and Performance

It's important to remember that technology is a tool to aid healthcare professionals and improve patient care. Therefore, the scalability and performance of these technologies should align with the practical needs and workflows of healthcare providers.

Collaboration and Continuous Improvement

Addressing scalability and performance issues is not a one-time task but a continuous process. It requires collaboration between technology developers, healthcare professionals, and regulatory bodies. Continuous monitoring, testing, and improvement are essential to ensure these technologies can meet the growing and evolving needs of the healthcare industry.

Preparing for the Future

As we prepare for a future where advanced technologies become an integral part of healthcare, addressing scalability and performance issues is essential. This preparation will not only involve technological advancements but also a rethinking of healthcare workflows and practices to integrate these technologies seamlessly.

Embracing the Challenges Ahead

Let's embrace these challenges as opportunities for innovation and growth. By focusing on scalability and performance, we can ensure that the integration of technologies like blockchain and AI in healthcare not only improves patient care but does so efficiently and sustainably.

The path ahead in making healthcare technology more scalable and high-performing is full of potential and promise. Let's continue on this path with a commitment to excellence, innovation, and a patient-centric approach, knowing that our efforts today will shape a better, more efficient healthcare system for the future

.

6 / legal and regulatory considerations

compliance with health regulations

LET'S pivot to an aspect that is the backbone of patient trust and safety: compliance with health regulations. Navigating the labyrinth of laws like HIPAA (Health Insurance Portability and Accountability Act) in the United States and GDPR (General Data Protection Regulation) in Europe is not just a legal obligation but a cornerstone of ethical healthcare practice.

Understanding HIPAA and GDPR

HIPAA and GDPR, though operating in different regions, share a common goal: protecting personal data, with a specific emphasis on health information. HIPAA sets the standard for protecting sensitive patient data in the U.S., while GDPR broadens the scope in the EU to include any personal data, offering individuals more control over their information.

The Significance of Compliance

Compliance is not merely about avoiding legal penalties; it's about building and maintaining patient trust. In an era where data breaches are alarmingly common, adhering to these regulations reassures patients that their sensitive health information is being handled with the utmost care and respect.

The Challenges of Compliance

Navigating these regulations can be a daunting task. They are comprehensive, detailed, and often subject to interpretation. Additionally, as technology evolves, so do the complexities of maintaining compliance. For example, the integration of blockchain in healthcare presents new questions about data ownership and consent under these regulations.

HIPAA: More Than Just Privacy Rules

HIPAA comprises several rules, including the Privacy Rule, which governs the use and disclosure of individuals' health information, and the Security Rule, which sets standards for securing electronic protected health information. Understanding and implementing these rules requires a multifaceted approach.

GDPR: Broadening the Horizon

GDPR, on the other hand, has a broader application. It affects any entity that processes the personal data of EU citizens, regardless of where the entity is based. GDPR emphasizes consent, data minimization, and the right of individuals to access their data, which poses unique challenges in healthcare data management.

Training and Awareness

One of the critical steps in ensuring compliance is training and awareness. Healthcare providers and staff must be educated about the nuances of these regulations and how they apply to their daily operations. This training should be ongoing, reflecting changes in both technology and legislation.

Data Protection Officers

For many organizations, appointing a Data Protection Officer (DPO) is a requirement under GDPR and a best practice under HIPAA. This role involves overseeing data protection strategy and ensuring compliance with the regulations.

Conducting Risk Assessments

Regular risk assessments are essential to identify potential areas of non-compliance. These assessments should be thorough, covering all aspects of data handling, from collection to processing to storage.

Implementing Robust Security Measures

Both HIPAA and GDPR require entities to implement appropriate security measures to protect data. This includes technical measures like encryption and pseudonymization, as well as organizational measures like access controls and data breach response plans.

Managing Third-Party Risks

Third-party vendors who handle health data on behalf of healthcare organizations also need to be compliant. This requires rigorous vetting processes and binding agreements to ensure that these third parties adhere to the same standards of data protection.

The Role of Technology in Compliance

Emerging technologies, while introducing complexity, also offer solutions for compliance. Blockchain can provide a secure and immutable record of data transactions, aiding in transparency and auditability. AI can be used to monitor data handling practices and identify potential breaches or non-compliance.

Handling Data Breaches

Even with the best precautions, data breaches can occur. Both HIPAA and GDPR have specific requirements for handling breaches, including timely notification to affected individuals and authorities. Having a robust breach response plan is critical.

Navigating International Compliance

For organizations operating internationally, navigating the compliance landscape becomes even more complex. They must ensure adherence not only to HIPAA and GDPR but also to other regional data protection laws, which can vary significantly.

Continuous Adaptation and Improvement

Compliance is not a static goal but a dynamic process. As regulations evolve and technology advances, healthcare organizations must continually adapt their practices and policies to stay compliant.

The Ethical Dimension of Compliance

Lastly, it's important to remember that at the heart of these regulations is the ethical imperative to protect patient privacy and data. Compliance, therefore, should be viewed not just as a legal requirement but as a moral duty to uphold the trust patients place in healthcare providers.

legal challenges in blockchain adoption

Now let's turn to a critical yet often overlooked aspect: the legal challenges surrounding the adoption of blockchain technology. As we've seen, blockchain holds tremendous potential for transforming healthcare, but its path is not without legal hurdles.

Navigating Uncharted Legal Territories

Blockchain technology is relatively new and evolving rapidly. One of the primary legal challenges is that the current legal framework in many jurisdictions is not fully equipped to address the unique attributes of blockchain technology. This gap between technology and law creates a landscape of uncertainty.

Understanding the Legal Implications of Decentralization

The decentralized nature of blockchain poses a significant legal challenge. Traditional legal systems are built around central authority and clear lines of responsibility, but blockchain disperses these across a network. This decentralization raises questions about jurisdiction: which laws apply, and in which country, when a blockchain spans the globe?

Data Privacy and Blockchain

Privacy laws, such as GDPR, pose specific challenges for blockchain technology. The immutable nature of blockchain seems to conflict with the GDPR principles, such as the right to be forgotten. Once data is entered into a blockchain, it cannot be altered or deleted, which could potentially violate these privacy rights.

Smart Contracts: Legal Status and Enforceability

Smart contracts, a cornerstone of blockchain's utility, also present legal challenges. There's an ongoing debate about their legal status: Are they legally binding contracts in the traditional sense, or do they represent a new category of agreements? The enforceability of smart contracts in a court of law is still a gray area that needs clarification.

Regulatory Compliance

Another challenge is ensuring that blockchain applications in healthcare are compliant with existing regulations, such as HIPAA in the US and GDPR in

Europe. These regulations have stringent requirements for data security and privacy, and navigating them in the context of blockchain technology is complex.

Intellectual Property Issues

Blockchain technology also raises questions about intellectual property rights. Who owns the data on a blockchain? Who owns the blockchain itself, especially when it's built and maintained by a network of users? These are vital questions in healthcare, where patient data and proprietary information are at play.

Liability in a Decentralized System

Determining liability in a decentralized system like blockchain is complicated. If something goes wrong – for instance, if a patient's data is mishandled or a smart contract malfunction leads to a loss – who is responsible? The absence of a central authority in blockchain networks makes this a challenging question.

The Challenge of Changing Regulations

Blockchain technology is evolving rapidly, and so is the regulatory landscape around it. Keeping up with these changes and ensuring compliance can be a daunting task for healthcare organizations.

Cross-border Transactions

Blockchain networks often operate across borders, which brings the challenge of dealing with multiple legal jurisdictions. Each country has its own set of laws and regulations, and a blockchain network must comply with all of these in cross-border transactions.

Standardization and Legal Uniformity

One way to address these legal challenges is through standardization. Developing standardized protocols and legal frameworks that can be universally applied to blockchain technologies could provide clarity and consistency.

Collaboration Between Technologists and Legal Experts

Addressing these legal challenges requires collaboration between technologists, legal experts, and regulators. It's essential to bridge the gap between the rapid pace of technological innovation and the more deliberate pace of legal and regulatory change.

Educating Stakeholders

Education plays a crucial role in navigating the legal landscape of blockchain technology. Stakeholders in the healthcare sector, from providers to patients, need to be educated about the legal implications of using blockchain technology.

The Role of Pilot Programs and Case Studies

Pilot programs and case studies can also be valuable in understanding and addressing the legal challenges of blockchain in healthcare. These real-world applications can provide insights into how blockchain technology interacts with existing legal frameworks.

international standards and policies

As we delve deeper, let's shift our focus to a broader canvas: international standards and policies. In an increasingly interconnected world, understanding the global landscape of standards and policies becomes essential, especially when navigating the complex realms of healthcare and technology.

The Globalized Nature of Healthcare

The healthcare industry is no longer confined within national borders. With the rise of telemedicine, international pharmaceutical supply chains, and cross-border data sharing, healthcare has become a global issue. This globalization necessitates a thorough understanding of international standards and policies.

Diverse Healthcare Policies Across Borders

Healthcare policies vary widely across countries. Each country has its own set of regulations governing healthcare delivery, data protection, and patient privacy. For instance, the U.S. has HIPAA, while the European Union has GDPR. Navigating these diverse policies is crucial for any healthcare provider or technology company operating on an international scale.

The Challenge of Standardization

One of the significant challenges in international healthcare is the lack of standardization. Different countries have different standards for healthcare quality, data management, and technology use. This lack of uniformity can lead to difficulties in ensuring consistent quality of care and data security across borders.

Data Privacy and Cross-Border Data Transfer

Data privacy is a critical issue in international healthcare. Different countries have different laws and regulations about how patient data can be collected, stored, and shared. For example, transferring patient data from a country under GDPR to a non-GDP compliant country involves navigating a complex web of legal requirements.

The Role of WHO and Other International Bodies

Organizations like the World Health Organization (WHO) play a significant role in setting international healthcare standards. They provide guidelines and frameworks that can help countries develop and refine their healthcare policies. However, the implementation of these guidelines varies from country to country.

International Standards for Medical Devices and Pharmaceuticals

For medical devices and pharmaceuticals, international standards are crucial for ensuring safety and efficacy. Organizations like the International Organization for Standardization (ISO) and the International Electrotechnical Commission (IEC) set these standards. Adhering to these standards is essential for any product that is marketed internationally.

The Impact of Technology on International Healthcare Policies

The rapid advancement of technology poses new challenges for international healthcare policies. Technologies like AI, blockchain, and telemedicine are evolving faster than the regulatory frameworks that govern them. This discrepancy can lead to legal and ethical challenges, particularly in cross-border scenarios.

Harmonizing Regulations for Telemedicine

Telemedicine is a prime example of a healthcare service that requires harmonization of international policies. As telemedicine knows no borders, it raises questions about licensure, quality of care, and data protection across different jurisdictions.

Emerging Technologies and Intellectual Property Laws

Intellectual property laws also play a crucial role in healthcare, especially when it comes to emerging technologies. Protecting intellectual property while ensuring that life-saving technologies are accessible to those who need them is a delicate balance that needs to be maintained.

Compliance with International Clinical Trial Standards

For clinical trials, compliance with international standards is crucial. This includes adhering to the International Council for Harmonisation of Technical Requirements for Pharmaceuticals for Human Use (ICH) guidelines, which set the standard for the design, conduct, safety, and reporting of clinical trials.

The Role of Bilateral and Multilateral Agreements

Bilateral and multilateral agreements between countries can help in standardizing healthcare practices and policies. These agreements can cover various aspects of healthcare, from research collaboration to data sharing, and can help in harmonizing healthcare standards across borders.

The Future of International Healthcare Policies

Looking ahead, the landscape of international healthcare policies is likely to evolve continuously. As new technologies emerge and global health challenges like pandemics arise, international cooperation and policy development will become even more critical.

Navigating the Future with Collaborative Efforts

Navigating this future will require collaborative efforts from governments, healthcare providers, technology companies, and international organizations. It will involve continuous dialogue, shared learning, and joint efforts to develop policies that are responsive to the changing landscape of global healthcare.

7 / challenges and limitations of blockchain in healthcare

technical limitations and challenges

WHILE TECHNOLOGY HAS UNDOUBTEDLY REVOLUTIONIZED healthcare, it's not without its hurdles. Let's unpack these challenges to gain a fuller understanding of the landscape we navigate.

1. The Interoperability Hurdle

A major challenge in healthcare technology is interoperability – the ability of different systems and software to communicate and exchange data efficiently. Despite advances in technology, many healthcare systems still operate in silos, with incompatible software and data formats. This lack of seamless interaction can impede the flow of vital patient information, affecting the quality of care.

2. Data Security and Privacy Concerns

With the increasing digitization of health records, data security and privacy concerns have skyrocketed. Cybersecurity threats are a constant worry, as breaches can lead to sensitive patient data being compromised. Ensuring robust security protocols and constantly updating them against evolving cyber threats is a significant technical and resource-intensive challenge.

3. Scaling Blockchain in Healthcare

While blockchain has been heralded for its potential in healthcare, scaling it effectively remains a challenge. Blockchain networks, especially those using Proof of Work (PoW) consensus mechanisms, can face issues like slow transaction times and high energy consumption. Adapting blockchain to healthcare's varied and large-scale needs requires overcoming these scalability issues.

4. The Complexity of Artificial Intelligence

AI in healthcare, particularly in diagnostic and predictive analytics, is only as good as the data it's fed. The challenge lies in not only having a large volume of data but ensuring the data is high-quality, diverse, and unbiased. Additionally, the 'black box' nature of AI algorithms can make it difficult for healthcare professionals to understand how AI reaches its conclusions, raising trust and ethical concerns.

5. Integration with Legacy Systems

Many healthcare facilities operate on legacy systems that are deeply entrenched and may not be compatible with newer technologies. Upgrading these systems can be costly and disruptive. The challenge lies in integrating advanced technologies like AI and blockchain with these older systems without causing operational disruptions.

6. Resource Constraints and Technological Divide

Resource constraints are a major barrier, especially in developing countries. Limited access to advanced technology, inadequate infrastructure, and a lack of skilled professionals can widen the technological divide, leading to disparities in healthcare quality and access.

7. Managing Big Data

The era of big data in healthcare brings its own set of challenges. Storing, managing, and analyzing vast amounts of data require sophisticated infrastructure and tools. Ensuring the accuracy and relevance of this data for patient care and research while maintaining privacy is a delicate balancing act.

8. Dependence on Network and Internet Connectivity

The efficacy of digital health solutions, including telemedicine and mobile health apps, is heavily reliant on network and internet connectivity. In areas with poor connectivity, this dependence can limit the accessibility and effectiveness of these solutions.

9. User Resistance and Change Management

Technological advancements often face resistance from users accustomed to traditional ways of working. Change management is a critical aspect, requiring education, training, and a gradual transition to new systems to ensure user buy-in and effective adoption.

10. Regulatory Compliance

Ensuring compliance with various regulatory standards can be technically challenging. Technologies must be adaptable to comply with different regulations across regions, which can be complex and time-consuming.

11. The Continual Evolution of Technology

The rapid pace of technological evolution means that healthcare technologies can quickly become outdated. Keeping up with these advancements, continually upgrading systems, and training staff on new technologies is a persistent challenge.

12. Reliability and Downtime

Reliability is crucial in healthcare technology. Systems failures and downtime can have serious implications for patient care. Ensuring high reliability and minimum downtime while maintaining and upgrading systems is a significant technical challenge.

13. Ethical Considerations in AI and Data Usage

Finally, ethical considerations in the use of AI and patient data remain a complex challenge. Balancing the benefits of predictive analytics and personalized medicine with ethical concerns around consent, data usage, and AI decision-making is a nuanced and ongoing conversation.

Embracing the Challenges as Opportunities

As we confront these technical limitations and challenges, it's important to view them as opportunities for growth and innovation. By acknowledging and addressing these hurdles head-on, we can pave the way for more robust, secure, and effective healthcare technologies.

organizational and cultural barriers

While technical challenges are often at the forefront, it's these human-centric factors that can truly make or break the successful implementation of technology in healthcare settings.

Understanding Organizational Dynamics

Every healthcare organization has its unique culture and dynamics. This encompasses a range of elements – from the hierarchy and decision-making processes to the attitudes and beliefs held by the staff. Implementing new technology in such a complex environment requires an understanding of these nuances.

Resistance to Change: A Human Nature

Resistance to change is a common human tendency and one of the primary barriers to technological adoption in healthcare. This resistance can stem from various factors, such as fear of the unknown, perceived threat to job security, or simply a preference for established routines.

The Generational Divide

In healthcare, there's often a generational divide in terms of technology adoption. While younger healthcare professionals may be more digitally savvy and open to technological innovations, older practitioners might prefer traditional methods. Bridging this gap requires patience, understanding, and tailored training programs.

Communication Gaps

Effective communication is vital for the successful implementation of new technologies. Often, there's a gap between those who develop the technology and those who use it. Healthcare professionals need clear, jargon-free explanations about how the technology works and its benefits to patient care.

Leadership's Role in Driving Change

Leadership plays a crucial role in overcoming organizational barriers. Leaders must not only advocate for new technologies but also actively participate in the change process. Their support can foster a culture of innovation and encourage staff to embrace new technologies.

Training and Education

A lack of adequate training and education is a significant barrier. Introducing new technology without proper training can lead to confusion, errors, and a reluctance to adopt the new system. Continuous education and hands-on training sessions are essential for smooth technological integration.

Workflow Disruptions

Introducing new technology can disrupt established workflows, leading to frustration among staff. It's important to anticipate these disruptions and plan for them. This might involve redesigning workflows or gradually phasing in the new technology.

The Power of Peer Influence

Peer influence can be a powerful tool in overcoming resistance. Healthcare professionals are more likely to embrace new technology if they see their peers successfully using it. Sharing success stories and positive experiences can help in building a supportive environment for change.

Cultural Sensitivity

Healthcare is a field that operates in diverse cultural contexts. Technologies need to be sensitive to these cultural differences. What works in one setting might not be suitable in another due to varying cultural norms and practices.

Balancing Technological and Human Aspects of Care

In the race to embrace technology, it's crucial not to lose sight of the human aspect of healthcare. Technologies should aid and enhance patient care, not replace the human touch that is fundamental to healthcare delivery.

Dealing with Burnout

Technology implementation can sometimes lead to burnout, especially if it adds to the workload of healthcare professionals. Recognizing the signs of burnout and addressing them promptly is crucial for the well-being of the staff and the success of technological integration.

Involving All Stakeholders

Successful technology integration requires the involvement of all stakeholders, from administrators to healthcare providers, and even patients. Gathering input from all these groups can provide valuable insights and foster a sense of ownership in the change process.

Evaluating and Adapting

Finally, it's important to continuously evaluate the impact of new technologies and be willing to adapt them based on feedback. This ongoing process of evaluation and adaptation can help in fine-tuning the technology to better fit the organizational culture and needs.

ethical considerations

It's imperative to address a vital component that underpins our journey: ethical considerations. The integration of technology in healthcare isn't just a matter of technical feasibility or regulatory compliance; it's also deeply entwined with a host of ethical issues. These are not merely academic concerns but are pivotal in shaping a healthcare system that is not only efficient but also compassionate and just.

The Ethical Landscape of Healthcare Technology

The healthcare sector, by its very nature, is grounded in ethics. From the Hippocratic Oath to modern-day ethical guidelines, the primary commitment has always been to do no harm and to prioritize patient welfare. However, as technology becomes increasingly integrated into healthcare, new ethical dimensions emerge.

Patient Privacy and Data Security

With the digitization of health records and the use of technologies like AI and blockchain, patient privacy and data security become paramount. It's not just about protecting data from breaches; it's about ensuring that sensitive health information isn't misused. The ethical obligation extends beyond legal compliance to a duty of maintaining patient trust.

Informed Consent in the Digital Age

Informed consent is a cornerstone of ethical medical practice. But what does informed consent look like in an era where patient data can be digitized, shared, and analyzed in ways that were previously unimaginable? Ensuring patients understand what they're consenting to in terms of data usage is a complex but crucial aspect.

Bias and Equity in AI

AI in healthcare presents its own set of ethical challenges. One of the most significant is the issue of bias. AI algorithms are only as unbiased as the data they're trained on. If this data is skewed, the AI's decisions and predictions may be biased, leading to unequal treatment of different patient groups.

Transparency and Explainability

There's also the challenge of transparency and explainability in AI systems. Healthcare decisions require accountability, but AI algorithms are often complex and not easily understood. Ensuring that AI decisions can be explained and justified is crucial for maintaining trust and accountability in healthcare decisions.

End-of-Life Care and Technological Interventions

Technological advancements have profoundly affected end-of-life care. The ability to sustain life through technology brings forth complex ethical questions. At what point does life-sustaining treatment become an undue burden? How do we balance technology's ability to prolong life with the patient's quality of life and dignity?

Genomics and Genetic Privacy

The field of genomics presents ethical dilemmas around genetic privacy and discrimination. As genetic testing becomes more prevalent, protecting individuals from discrimination based on their genetic information becomes a significant concern.

Resource Allocation and Access

With advanced healthcare technologies often comes a high cost. This raises ethical questions about resource allocation and access. Who gets access to these advanced treatments? How do we ensure equity in healthcare when some technologies are prohibitively expensive?

The Role of Healthcare Providers

Healthcare providers face ethical dilemmas in integrating technology into their practice. Balancing technological interventions with holistic patient care, preserving the human element in healthcare, and ensuring that technology enhances rather than replaces the provider-patient relationship are key considerations.

Cultural Sensitivity and Global Applications

Ethical considerations in healthcare technology also have a cultural dimension. Technologies need to be sensitive to cultural differences in healthcare beliefs and practices, especially when applied in a global context.

Future Challenges and Ongoing Dialogue

As technology continues to evolve, new ethical challenges will undoubtedly emerge. Staying ahead of these challenges requires an ongoing dialogue among healthcare providers, technologists, ethicists, and patients.

Ethics as a Guiding Principle

In this landscape of rapid technological advancement, it's crucial to keep ethics at the forefront of our discussions and decisions. Ethics should not be an afterthought but a guiding principle that shapes the development and implementation of healthcare technology.

8 / the future of blockchain in healthcare

emerging trends and future applications

ONE OF THE most exciting trends in healthcare is the shift towards personalized medicine. This approach tailors treatment to the individual characteristics of each patient, taking into account their genetic makeup, lifestyle, and environment. Technologies like genomics, AI, and big data analytics play pivotal roles in this shift, offering insights that can lead to more targeted and effective treatments.

AI and Machine Learning: The Next Frontier

Artificial Intelligence and machine learning continue to push the boundaries of what's possible in healthcare. From diagnostic algorithms that can detect diseases with greater accuracy than ever before to predictive analytics that can foresee patient risks and outcomes, AI is transforming the landscape of healthcare.

Blockchain Beyond Data Security

While we've extensively discussed blockchain in the context of data security and patient records, its potential applications go much further. Blockchain could revolutionize supply chain management, ensuring the authenticity and traceability of pharmaceuticals and medical supplies. It could also facilitate health information exchanges by creating a secure, interoperable platform for data sharing.

Wearable Technology and IoT

Wearable technology and the Internet of Things (IoT) are set to play increasingly significant roles in healthcare. These technologies are not just about tracking fitness; they're evolving into powerful tools for proactive health management. Wearables can monitor vital signs, detect abnormalities, and even administer medication, all while providing invaluable data for healthcare providers.

Telemedicine and Remote Care

The COVID-19 pandemic accelerated the adoption of telemedicine, but this is just the beginning. Future applications could include remote surgeries performed via robotic systems and more advanced telehealth platforms that offer a wider range of services, making healthcare more accessible to underserved populations.

3D Printing in Healthcare

3D printing technology is making strides in healthcare. From printing personalized prosthetics and orthopedic implants to bioprinting tissues and organs for transplant, the potential of 3D printing is vast and could significantly reduce waiting times for transplant patients and improve the compatibility of implants and prosthetics.

The Integration of Robotics

Robotics in healthcare is moving beyond surgical assistance. We are looking at a future where robots could play roles in patient care, rehabilitation, and even in providing companionship to the elderly. The blend of AI and robotics could lead to more autonomous systems capable of supporting both healthcare providers and patients in various ways.

Virtual Reality and Augmented Reality

Virtual Reality (VR) and Augmented Reality (AR) are finding applications in healthcare training, patient education, and therapy. VR simulations can provide immersive training environments for medical professionals, while AR can aid in complex surgeries by providing real-time, 3D visualizations of the patient's anatomy.

Ethical AI and Responsible Innovation

As technology continues to advance, the focus on ethical AI and responsible innovation becomes more critical. Ensuring that AI systems are transparent, unbiased, and respectful of privacy will be paramount. The goal is to harness the power of AI while maintaining ethical standards and human-centered care.

Challenges of Technological Integration

Despite these exciting trends, challenges remain, particularly in integrating these technologies into existing healthcare systems. Balancing innovation with practicality, cost, and accessibility will be key. Training healthcare professionals to adapt to these new technologies will also be essential.

The Importance of Patient-Centric Approaches

In all these technological advancements, the importance of maintaining a patient-centric approach cannot be overstated. Technology should enhance, not replace, the human aspect of healthcare. Ensuring that these technologies are used in a way that genuinely benefits patients will be the true measure of their success.

Preparing for the Future

As we look to the future, the possibilities are endless. But it's not just about the technology itself; it's about how we use it. It's about ensuring that these advancements lead to more equitable, efficient, and compassionate healthcare for all.

role of blockchain in pandemic response and global health

The COVID-19 pandemic has underscored the need for robust, efficient, and transparent systems in managing health crises. Let's delve into how blockchain technology can be a game-changer in this realm.

Blockchain: A Brief Refresher

Before we dive into the specifics, let's briefly recap what blockchain is. It's a decentralized ledger technology known for its security, transparency, and immutability. These features make it an attractive tool for various applications in healthcare, particularly in responding to pandemics and managing global health initiatives.

Enhancing Supply Chain Transparency and Efficiency

One of the most critical challenges during a pandemic is managing the supply chain for medical supplies and vaccines. Blockchain can enhance supply chain transparency and efficiency. It provides a real-time, tamper-proof record of supply movements, helping to prevent shortages, reduce waste, and identify bottlenecks. This feature became crucial during the COVID-19 pandemic for the distribution of personal protective equipment (PPE) and later, vaccines.

Streamlining Vaccine Distribution

In vaccine distribution, blockchain can track vaccine production, shipment, and delivery. This tracking ensures that vaccines are distributed efficiently and equitably. Moreover, it can help in monitoring storage conditions, especially for vaccines that require specific temperature settings.

Facilitating Secure Data Sharing for Research

Pandemic response requires global collaboration, particularly in research. Blockchain enables secure data sharing among researchers, healthcare professionals, and institutions. By creating a unified platform for data sharing, blockchain can accelerate research efforts, from understanding the disease to developing treatments and vaccines.

Contact Tracing and Privacy Concerns

Contact tracing is vital in managing pandemics, but it raises privacy concerns. Blockchain can offer a solution by providing a platform for contact tracing that respects individual privacy. Data can be anonymized and encrypted, ensuring that personal information is not compromised while still allowing for effective tracing and containment efforts.

Managing Health Records and Patient Data

During a pandemic, efficiently managing health records and patient data is more important than ever. Blockchain can facilitate this by creating decentralized databases for patient records, accessible to authorized healthcare providers. This system can be particularly beneficial in tracking the health status and treatment responses of patients on a large scale.

Global Health Initiatives and Blockchain

Beyond pandemics, blockchain has the potential to revolutionize various aspects of global health. In developing countries, where healthcare infrastructure might be lacking, blockchain can provide a secure and efficient way to manage health data, monitor disease outbreaks, and facilitate health interventions.

Fostering Transparency in International Aid

Blockchain can also play a role in managing international health aid. It can ensure that aid is distributed transparently and reaches its intended recipients, reducing the risk of fraud and corruption.

Challenges in Implementing Blockchain in Healthcare

Despite its potential, implementing blockchain in healthcare, particularly in pandemic response, is not without challenges. Issues such as interoperability with existing systems, scalability, and the digital divide (access to technology) are significant barriers that need to be addressed.

Ethical and Legal Considerations

Additionally, there are ethical and legal considerations. Ensuring that the use of blockchain in healthcare complies with regulations like HIPAA and GDPR, and addressing ethical concerns around data privacy and consent, are imperative.

Preparing for the Future

The COVID-19 pandemic has been a wake-up call about the need for more resilient healthcare systems. Blockchain technology offers promising solutions, but realizing its full potential requires collaboration across governments, healthcare organizations, technology companies, and international bodies.

The Path Ahead

As we look to the future, the role of blockchain in pandemic response and global health will likely become more prominent. By addressing the current challenges and continuing to innovate, blockchain can be a vital tool in building a more prepared and responsive healthcare system on a global scale.

vision for a blockchain-enabled healthcare system

Imagine a healthcare system where patient data is not stored in centralized databases vulnerable to breaches, but on a secure, decentralized blockchain. In this system, each patient has a unique digital identity linked to their medical records, accessible anywhere, anytime, by authorized personnel. This setup not only enhances data security but also ensures that patients have more control over their health information.

Streamlined Data Sharing and Collaboration

In our envisioned system, data sharing among healthcare providers, researchers, and policymakers is seamless and secure, thanks to blockchain. This interoperability facilitates collaboration, leading to more comprehensive care for patients and more robust research outcomes. A patient visiting a specialist, for instance, no longer needs to undergo repeat tests; their medical history, including tests and results, is readily available, reducing redundancy and saving time and resources.

Revolutionizing Supply Chain Management

The blockchain-enabled healthcare system revolutionizes supply chain management. Each pharmaceutical product and medical supply is tagged and tracked on the blockchain, offering real-time visibility and ensuring authenticity. This tracking system drastically reduces the chances of counterfeit medicines entering the supply chain and allows for efficient management of medical inventory.

Enhanced Security and Compliance

Blockchain inherently enhances security and compliance. With each transaction recorded on an immutable ledger, the system offers a transparent audit trail, ensuring adherence to regulatory standards such as HIPAA and GDPR. In this envisioned system, the challenges of compliance become more manageable, as blockchain provides a structured and secure framework for handling sensitive health data.

Empowering Patients with Smart Contracts

Smart contracts automate and streamline various healthcare processes. These could range from managing insurance claims to handling consent for medical procedures. Patients, for instance, could use smart contracts to grant temporary access to their health records for a specific treatment, enhancing their autonomy and control over their personal health information.

Predictive Analytics and Personalized Medicine

Integrating blockchain with AI and big data analytics paves the way for predictive healthcare and personalized medicine. In this system, health trends and disease patterns can be analyzed securely and efficiently, leading to early intervention strategies and customized treatment plans based on a patient's specific health profile.

Global Health Initiatives

On a global scale, blockchain enables more efficient management of health initiatives, particularly in resource-limited settings. It aids in tracking the distribution of resources, monitoring the spread of diseases, and ensuring that aid reaches its intended destination, all while maintaining data integrity and transparency.

Telemedicine and Remote Care

Blockchain also bolsters the growth of telemedicine. With secure and accessible patient data, remote consultations and treatments become more feasible and reliable. This aspect of the healthcare system is particularly beneficial for patients in remote or underserved areas, improving accessibility to quality healthcare services.

Challenges and Mitigation Strategies

While this vision is promising, it's not without challenges. Technical limitations, such as scalability and integration with existing systems, need to be addressed. Additionally, there's the need for a cultural shift in the healthcare industry towards adopting new technologies and the training required for healthcare professionals to adapt to these changes.

Ethical Considerations and Patient-Centric Care

Moreover, maintaining a patient-centric approach is paramount. The ethical considerations, particularly around data privacy and the digital divide, need to be at the forefront of this blockchain-enabled healthcare system. The goal is to leverage technology to enhance patient care, not to overshadow the human element that is the essence of healthcare.

9 / conclusion

summarizing the impact of blockchain on healthcare

ONE OF THE most significant impacts of blockchain in healthcare is the transformation of patient data management. Blockchain's decentralized nature ensures that patient data is not stored in a single location, thereby reducing the risks associated with centralized data storage, such as data breaches and unauthorized access. This system provides patients with greater control over their personal health information, enhancing patient privacy and security.

Enhancing Interoperability and Collaboration

Blockchain technology has the potential to greatly improve interoperability among different healthcare systems and platforms. By creating a standardized, secure platform for data exchange, blockchain facilitates better collaboration among healthcare providers. This enhanced interoperability leads to more comprehensive and coordinated patient care, as well as more efficient use of healthcare resources.

Streamlining Supply Chain Management

The impact of blockchain on the healthcare supply chain is profound. Blockchain provides a transparent and immutable record of the supply chain, from the manufacturing of pharmaceuticals and medical devices to their delivery to healthcare facilities and patients. This transparency helps in combating counterfeit drugs, managing inventory more effectively, and ensuring the timely distribution of medical supplies.

Automating Processes with Smart Contracts

Smart contracts, a vital feature of blockchain, automate numerous healthcare processes, including insurance claims processing, patient consent management, and compliance with regulatory requirements. This automation not only saves time and resources but also reduces the potential for human error and fraud.

Facilitating Research and Clinical Trials

Blockchain technology has a significant impact on medical research and clinical trials. It offers a secure and efficient way to manage and share research data, ensuring data integrity and confidentiality. This leads to faster and more reliable research outcomes, ultimately accelerating the development of new treatments and therapies.

Addressing Privacy and Security Concerns

In a world where data breaches are increasingly common, blockchain's robust security features address critical privacy and security concerns in healthcare. The encryption and immutability of blockchain provide an added layer of security to patient data, reinforcing patient trust in the healthcare system.

Challenges in Implementation

Despite these benefits, the implementation of blockchain in healthcare is not without its challenges. Technical issues such as scalability, integration with existing IT systems, and the need for a skilled workforce are significant hurdles. Additionally, there are legal and regulatory challenges to navigate, especially concerning patient data privacy and the use of blockchain technology across different jurisdictions.

The Ethical Dimension

Ethical considerations, particularly in terms of equitable access to technology and the potential misuse of patient data, are crucial in the adoption of blockchain in healthcare. Ensuring that the benefits of blockchain are accessible to all, and that the technology is used in an ethical and responsible manner, is imperative.

Future Outlook

Looking to the future, the impact of blockchain on

healthcare is poised to grow. As the technology evolves and as more stakeholders in the healthcare industry embrace blockchain, its potential to transform healthcare becomes increasingly evident. From personalized medicine and improved patient outcomes to more efficient healthcare systems and reduced costs, the possibilities are vast and promising.

Embracing the Change

As we conclude this exploration, it's clear that blockchain technology represents a paradigm shift in healthcare. Embracing this change requires not only technological innovation but also a cultural shift within the healthcare industry. It demands collaboration among healthcare providers, technology experts, policymakers, and patients.

Final Thoughts

Blockchain technology, with its unique features and potential applications, is set to redefine the landscape of healthcare. By addressing the challenges and harnessing the benefits, we can unlock a future where healthcare is more secure, efficient, and patient-centered. Let's move forward with a commitment to continuous learning and innovation, with the goal of leveraging blockchain technology to create a better healthcare system for all.

key takeaways

As we reflect on the various themes and discussions we've navigated, let's distill the essence of our exploration into key takeaways that encapsulate the core learnings and insights.

1. Blockchain as a Catalyst for Transformation in Healthcare

Our exploration began with understanding blockchain as not just a technology, but as a catalyst for profound transformation in healthcare. Its decentralized nature, immutability, and transparency offer a new paradigm for managing healthcare data, enhancing patient privacy, and improving the integrity of healthcare processes.

2. Enhanced Data Management and Security

One of the most significant impacts of blockchain in healthcare is on data management and security. The ability of blockchain to securely manage patient records, ensure data integrity, and facilitate controlled access to health information stands as a cornerstone for advancing patient care and trust in the healthcare system.

3. Improved Interoperability and Efficient Healthcare Delivery

Blockchain's potential to improve interoperability among different healthcare systems is pivotal. By enabling seamless and secure data exchange, blockchain can lead to more coordinated and efficient healthcare delivery, reducing redundancies and enhancing the quality of patient care.

4. The Role of Smart Contracts in Streamlining Processes

Smart contracts emerged as a vital aspect of blockchain in healthcare. These self-executing contracts have the potential to automate complex processes, from insurance claims to patient consent, thereby increasing efficiency and reducing administrative burdens in healthcare systems.

5. Overcoming Technical and Scalability Challenges

We recognized that while blockchain presents numerous opportunities, it is not without its challenges. Technical issues such as scalability, energy consumption, and integration with existing IT infrastructure pose significant hurdles that need addressing for blockchain to achieve its full potential in healthcare.

6. Tackling Legal and Regulatory Hurdles

The legal and regulatory landscape for blockchain in healthcare is complex and evolving. Navigating this landscape requires a deep understanding of laws like HIPAA and GDPR, and a commitment to ensuring that blockchain applications in healthcare comply with these regulations while respecting patient privacy and rights.

7. Ethical Considerations Are Paramount

Our discussions underscored the importance of ethical considerations in implementing blockchain in healthcare. Balancing technological advancement with ethical implications, particularly in terms of data privacy, consent, and equitable access to technology, is essential.

8. The Global Impact and Future Applications

Looking globally, blockchain has the potential to impact various aspects of healthcare, from pandemic response to global health initiatives. Its application can lead to more transparent and efficient management of health resources, especially in underserved or resource-limited areas.

9. The Human Element Remains Central

In all our discussions, one theme remained constant: the primacy of the human element in healthcare. Technology, no matter how advanced, should augment and not replace the human touch that is fundamental to patient care.

10. Continuous Learning and Adaptation

The field of blockchain in healthcare is dynamic and rapidly evolving. Staying abreast of technological advancements, continuously learning, and adapting to new information and tools will be crucial for healthcare professionals and organizations.

11. Collaboration Across Disciplines

The integration of blockchain into healthcare is not just a technological endeavor but a collaborative one. It requires concerted efforts from healthcare professionals, technologists, policymakers, legal experts, and patients. Such multi-disciplinary collaboration can drive innovation and ensure that the technology is used in a way that benefits all stakeholders.

12. Preparing for a Blockchain-Enabled Future

As we prepare for a future where blockchain becomes an integral part of the healthcare landscape, embracing change, fostering innovation, and prioritizing patient-centered care will be key. This preparation involves not only technological adoption but also cultural and organizational shifts within the healthcare sector.

call to action for healthcare stakeholders

The healthcare sector stands at a crossroads. The challenges of managing patient data, ensuring privacy, streamlining operations, and improving patient outcomes are more pressing than ever. Blockchain technology presents a promising solution, but realizing its potential requires concerted action from all stakeholders.

Healthcare Professionals: Embrace and Advocate

For healthcare professionals, the first step is embracing the change. Understand the potential of blockchain and how it can enhance patient care and healthcare operations. Become an advocate for technology adoption in your workplace. Seek out training and educational resources to familiarize yourself with the nuances of blockchain technology.

Staying Ahead of the Curve

Continuous learning is key. The healthcare landscape is rapidly evolving, and staying abreast of the latest technological advancements, including blockchain, is vital. Attend workshops, seminars, and conferences. Engage with professional communities that focus on healthcare technology.

Policymakers: Foster a Conducive Environment

Policymakers play a crucial role in shaping the adoption of blockchain in healthcare. This involves creating a regulatory framework that encourages innovation while ensuring patient safety and data privacy. It's about striking a balance between regulation and innovation.

Encouraging Research and Development

Support research and development in blockchain technology for healthcare applications. Provide funding and resources for pilot projects that explore the practical applications of blockchain in healthcare settings.

Technologists: Collaborate and Innovate

For technologists and blockchain developers, the call to action is to collaborate closely with healthcare professionals. Understand their needs, challenges, and workflows. Develop solutions that are not just technologically advanced but also user-friendly, practical, and easily integrable into existing healthcare systems.

Prioritize Security and Ethics

In developing blockchain solutions, prioritize security and ethical considerations. Understand the sensitivities around patient data and ensure that your solutions comply with healthcare regulations and ethical standards.

Patients: Get Involved and Stay Informed

Patients are at the heart of the healthcare system. Stay informed about how technology, especially blockchain, can impact your healthcare experience. Be proactive in understanding how your data is managed and used.

Advocate for Transparency and Control

Advocate for greater transparency and control over your health data. Engage with your healthcare providers to understand how they are using technology to secure and manage your health information.

Healthcare Institutions: Lead the Way

Healthcare institutions have the power to lead the transformation. Invest in blockchain technology infrastructure. Foster a culture of innovation within your organization.

Implement Training and Change Management Programs

Implement comprehensive training and change management programs to facilitate the smooth integration of blockchain technology. It's essential for staff at all levels to understand and be comfortable with the new technology.

Promote Interdisciplinary Collaboration

Encourage interdisciplinary collaboration within the organization. Blockchain technology intersects various fields - from IT to healthcare to legal. Fostering a collaborative environment is crucial for holistic and successful implementation.

Insurance Companies: Adapt and Innovate

For insurance companies, the adoption of blockchain presents an opportunity to streamline operations, reduce fraud, and improve customer satisfaction. Explore how blockchain can automate claims processing and enhance data security.

Research and Academic Institutions: Educate and Explore

Academic and research institutions should integrate blockchain technology into their curricula and research programs. Educate the next generation of healthcare professionals about this technology and explore new research avenues in blockchain applications in healthcare.

10 / appendices

glossary of blockchain and healthcare terms

1. Blockchain: At its core, blockchain is a decentralized digital ledger technology. Each 'block' in the chain contains a number of transactions, and every new transaction added to the blockchain is recorded across each copy of the ledger distributed over numerous computers. This makes the data highly resistant to tampering.

2. Decentralization: This refers to the distribution of functions and powers away from a central location or authority. In blockchain, decentralization means that no single entity has control over the entire chain of data, enhancing security and transparency.

3. Smart Contracts: Self-executing contracts with the terms of the agreement written directly into lines of code.

They automatically perform certain actions when predefined conditions are met, without the need for intermediaries.

4. Interoperability: In healthcare, interoperability is the ability of different information systems, devices, and applications to access, exchange, integrate, and cooperatively use data in a coordinated manner, within and across organizational boundaries.

5. HIPAA (Health Insurance Portability and Accountability Act): A U.S. law designed to provide privacy standards to protect patients' medical records and other health information provided to health plans, doctors, hospitals, and other healthcare providers.

6. GDPR (General Data Protection Regulation): A regulation in EU law on data protection and privacy in the European Union and the European Economic Area. It also addresses the transfer of personal data outside the EU and EEA areas.

7. Cryptography: The practice and study of techniques for secure communication in the presence of third parties called adversaries. Blockchain utilizes cryptographic algorithms to secure data.

8. Consensus Mechanism: A process in blockchain technology used to achieve agreement on a single data value among distributed processes or systems. Proof of Work (PoW) and Proof of Stake (PoS) are common consensus mechanisms.

9. Immutability: The ability of the blockchain to remain unaltered and indelible. Once data has been written to a blockchain, it is virtually impossible to change it.

10. Distributed Ledger Technology (DLT): A consensus of replicated, shared, and synchronized digital data spread across multiple sites, countries, or institutions. There is no central administrator or centralized data storage.

11. Tokenization: The process of substituting sensitive data with unique identification symbols that retain all the essential information without compromising its security.

12. Nodes: In blockchain, a node is any computing device (computer, phone, etc.) that is participating in the network by maintaining a copy of the ledger and, in some cases, processes transactions.

13. Digital Identity: A digital representation of an individual's identity, which in healthcare can be used to represent a patient's health records and personal health information.

14. Supply Chain Management: In healthcare, this involves overseeing the entire lifecycle of a medical product, from production to distribution to consumption. Blockchain can enhance transparency and traceability in this process.

15. Data Encryption: The method of converting plaintext into a secret code or cipher text to prevent unauthorized access. It's a critical aspect of securing patient data in healthcare.

16. Telemedicine: The use of electronic information and telecommunication technologies to provide and support healthcare when distance separates the participants.

17. Electronic Health Records (EHRs): Digital versions of patients' paper charts. EHRs are real-time, patient-centered records that make information available instantly and securely to authorized users.

18. Compliance: In healthcare, compliance involves adhering to laws, regulations, guidelines, and specifications relevant to the industry. Blockchain can help in maintaining compliance, especially with regulations like HIPAA and GDPR.

19. Public and Private Blockchain: A public blockchain is one where anyone can join and participate in the network, while a private blockchain restricts the participation to selected entities.

20. Health Information Exchange (HIE): The electronic movement of health-related information among organizations according to nationally recognized standards.

resources for further reading and research

Academic Journals and Publications

- Journal of Biomedical Informatics: A respected journal that frequently publishes articles on the use of blockchain in healthcare.

- Blockchain in Healthcare Today: The first peer-reviewed journal that amplifies and disseminates distributed ledger technology research and innovations in the healthcare sector.

- Health Affairs: While not solely focused on blockchain, this journal often features articles on health policy and technology innovations, including blockchain applications in healthcare.

Online Courses and Educational Platforms

- Coursera and edX: These platforms offer various courses on blockchain technology, including applications in healthcare.

- Udemy: Offers beginner to advanced courses focused on blockchain, helping professionals understand the underlying mechanisms and applications.

Research Institutions and Think Tanks

- MIT Media Lab's Digital Currency Initiative: Engages in research and provides thought leadership on digital currencies and blockchain technology.

- The Brookings Institution: Frequently publishes research and analysis on the impact of blockchain technology on various sectors, including healthcare.

Industry Reports and White Papers

- Deloitte's Insights: Offers numerous white papers and industry reports on blockchain technology in healthcare, detailing current trends, challenges, and future potential.

- McKinsey & Company Reports: Provides analysis on

how blockchain technology is shaping various industries, including the health sector.

Conferences and Workshops

- Healthcare Information and Management Systems Society (HIMSS) Conference: An annual event where healthcare professionals can learn about the latest in healthcare technology, including blockchain.

- Blockchain in Healthcare Symposium: A global conference that focuses on the implementation of blockchain in the healthcare sector.

Online Forums and Discussion Groups

- LinkedIn Groups: There are various LinkedIn groups dedicated to blockchain in healthcare where professionals share insights, news, and discussions.

- Reddit Communities: Subreddits like r/healthcare and r/blockchain are platforms for discussion and sharing of information about the latest developments in the field.

Governmental and Regulatory Bodies

- U.S. Food and Drug Administration (FDA): Provides information on regulatory policies regarding the use of blockchain in healthcare.

- European Commission's Digital Health and Blockchain Technology: Offers insights into how the European Union is approaching blockchain in healthcare.

Blogs and Websites

- CoinDesk and Cointelegraph: While primarily

focused on cryptocurrency, these websites also cover the broader applications of blockchain, including healthcare.

- HealthIT.gov: Offers resources and information on the latest technologies in healthcare, including blockchain applications.

Podcasts and Webinars

- Healthcare IT Today: This podcast often covers topics related to emerging technologies in healthcare, including blockchain.

- Blockchain in Healthcare Today Webinars: Offers a series of webinars featuring experts discussing the role of blockchain in the healthcare sector.

www.ingramcontent.com/pod-product-compliance
Lightning Source LLC
LaVergne TN
LVHW090419210926
848480LV00002B/618